Date: 01/30/12

SAVE THE
ORANGUTAN

Sarah Eason

PowerKiDS
press.

New York

Published in 2009 by The Rosen Publishing Group, Inc.
29 East 21st Street, New York, NY 10010

Illustrators: Andrew Geeson and Marijke Van Veldhoven
Designer: Paul Myerscough
Consultant: Michael Scott
U.S. Editor: Kara Murray

Photo Credits: Ardea/Jean Paul Ferrero p. 9 /Masahiro Lijima front cover; Corbis/Chaiwat Subprasom/Reuters p. 7; Dreamstime p. 17 /Eric Gevaert p. 23, p. 25 /Ratnakar Krothapalli p. 26 /Rommel Rondario p. 24 /Gary Unwin p. 27 /Christopher Waters p. 14; FLPA/Simon Hosking p. 18; istockphoto p. 4, p. 5, p. 6R, p. 8, p. 12, p. 13, p. 15, p. 21, p. 22; Photos.com p. 6L; Shutterstock/Norma Cornes p. 20 /Brandon Mayoral p. 16 /David McKee poster /Adrian Phillips p. 19 /TAOLMOR p. 11 /Andy Z p. 10 /A.S. Zain p. 28, p. 29.

Library of Congress Cataloging-in-Publication Data

Eason, Sarah.
 Save the orangutan / Sarah Eason. — 1st ed.
     p. cm. — (Save the)
 Includes index.
 ISBN 978-1-4358-2811-7 (library binding)
 1. Orangutan—Juvenile literature. I. Title.
 QL737.P96E24 2009
 599.88'3—dc22

                          2008024481

Printed in China

Contents

Why Are Orangutans So Special?

After humans, orangutans are the most intelligent animals on Earth. They are also one of our closest **relatives**. Orangutans are so much like us that the **native** people who live near them call them *Orang Hutan*, which means "people of the forest."

SAVE THE ORANGUTAN!

There are many things that you can do to help save the orangutan. Look out for the Save the Orangutan boxes in this book for ways in which you and your friends can help.

The orangutan is an ape. It is the only ape that lives in Asia. All other apes live in Africa. Orangutans are the biggest tree-living animals in the world. Although they are large animals, they can swing easily through the treetops in which they live.

I have long arms and legs. I use them to reach branches as I swing through trees.

I can live to be 50 years old.

North America

Europe

Asia

Africa

South America

Sumatra

Borneo

Australia

We live on just two islands in Asia. The islands are called Sumatra and Borneo. The islands are marked in red on this map of the world.

Did You Know?

Orangutans live in treetops 98 feet (30 m) above the ground.

Why Are Orangutans in Danger?

Just 10 years fro

Rainforests in which orangutans live are under threat. Rainforest trees are cut down for wood and land is cleared to make way for farms and houses. Almost 80 percent of rainforests that were orangutan homes have now been destroyed.

destroyed rainforest

Rainforest trees are also cut down to make paper and furniture. That leaves very little forest in which orangutans can live.

We are sometimes taken from the wild and sold to perform in circuses.

ow, orangutans may be extinct.

Sometimes, baby orangutans are kept as pets. To capture a baby, hunters must first kill its mother. Many captured babies die of shock.

Did You Know?

An area of rainforest the size of four soccer fields is destroyed every minute.

Where Do Orangutans Live?

Orangutans live in the rainforests of two islands called Borneo and Sumatra. Orangutans live high up in the treetops – they even sleep there. By living in treetops, orangutans keep safe from **predators** on the forest floor.

SAVE THE ORANGUTAN!

Help protect rainforests. Only buy furniture made from wood approved by wildlife-protection organizations.

Adult orangutans live mostly alone. They must eat a lot of fruit every day to stay alive. Each orangutan needs a large area of rainforest to itself in order to find enough food.

Did You Know?

45,000 orangutans live on Borneo. 7,000 live on Sumatra.

At night I sleep in a nest high up in the trees. I make a new nest every night by bending and weaving together twigs and branches.

Many amazing animals live in our rainforest home.

Tigers, leopards and even large pythons hunt orangutans.

What Do Orangutans Look Like?

Orangutans, chimpanzees, gorillas and bonobos belong to an animal group called great apes. **Scientists** say people are so like these great apes that we are part of the same animal group. Orangutans have ears, eyes and hands that are very much like ours.

Sumatran orangutans have much longer hair than Bornean orangutans.

I can walk short distances. I walk on all fours.

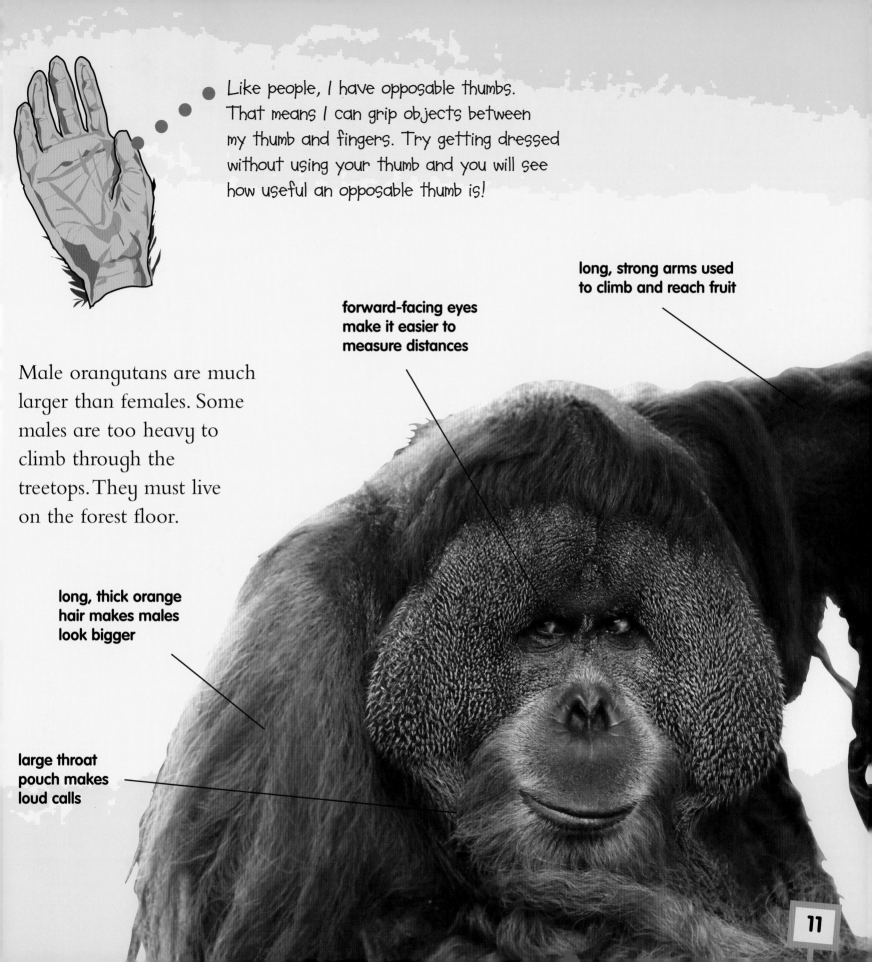

Like people, I have opposable thumbs. That means I can grip objects between my thumb and fingers. Try getting dressed without using your thumb and you will see how useful an opposable thumb is!

long, strong arms used to climb and reach fruit

forward-facing eyes make it easier to measure distances

Male orangutans are much larger than females. Some males are too heavy to climb through the treetops. They must live on the forest floor.

long, thick orange hair makes males look bigger

large throat pouch makes loud calls

What Do Orangutans Eat?

Orangutans spend many hours each day searching for tasty things to eat. They are mainly **vegetarian** and eat all kinds of leaves, nuts, seeds and **fungi**. Orangutans even eat tree bark! Orangutans love honey and **flower nectar**, but nothing beats fruit – their favorite food.

YUM, YUM

Long rainy seasons, call

SAVE THE ORANGUTAN!

Orangutans need plenty of fruit trees to survive. Help them by **joining an** environmental group **that protects** rainforests.

Orangutans help keep the rainforests alive. Fruit seeds inside their droppings grow into new trees on the forest floor.

I rarely eat meat, but I sometimes eat a few small **mammals**, insects or bird's eggs. If I'm lucky, I might find a **termite** nest. Delicious!

onsoons, help the forest trees grow the fruit we eat.

This is my favorite fruit. It is called a durian. It smells horrible, but it tastes deliciously sweet.

Did You Know?

90 percent of my food is fruit.

What Do Orangutans Do All Day?

Orangutans wake at dawn. They leave their nests and travel across a huge area looking for food. From time to time, the rainforest explodes with fruit. Although orangutans normally live alone, they gather together at these times to eat and show off!

Sometime

Did You Know?

I can spend up to six hours a day looking for food and eating.

Orangutans leave their mothers when they become young adults. They sometimes then live with another mother and her baby for a while, to make the separation from their own mother easier.

When I meet other young orangutans, I get very excited. We have fun wrestling and playing together.

like to just sit and watch the world go by!

In the early afternoon, I make myself a day nest, where I can have a nap. My day nest is much smaller than my night nest.

How Do Orangutans Talk?

Orangutans use lots of sounds and movements to talk to each other. They also make different faces to show how they are feeling. Many of the faces that orangutans make are like those made by people.

SAVE THE ORANGUTAN!

Go to the Web site www.rainforest.org for ways you can help protect the rainforest.

Orangutans can make a noise by pursing their lips and blowing air out of their mouths. If you annoy one, it might blow a raspberry at you!

Did You Know?

A male orangutan's call lasts for up to three minutes!

I am a male orangutan. I make a loud, booming call by puffing up my throat pouch and roaring. This warns other males to stay out of my **territory**.

When I am happy, I smile – just like you.

I am a male oranguatan. I protect my rainforest area by making a sound called a fast call to show that I am tough and able to fight. I also show how big my teeth are to scare other males away.

Are Orangutans Intelligent?

Orangutans are very intelligent. Like people, they have a large skull to protect their big brains. Orangutans are very good at solving problems. They sometimes escape from zoos by taking apart fences and taking hinges off metal doors!

Look at me!

I remembe

I am too clever to be kept in a cage. My zookeeper has dug a deep **moat** around my pen to stop me from escaping, but I can make a bridge out of branches to cross it!

I can't speak like a person, but I can talk to you with sign language. I can even teach sign language to other orangutans!

Did You Know?

The number of orangutans in the wild has been halved in the last 60 years.

Orangutans use sticks to dig honey out of bees' nests or to poke insects out of holes. They use leaves as a glove to pick up prickly fruit. They can even make a hat to shelter themselves from rain.

hings well and I learn very quickly.

How Do Orangutans Find a Mate?

Orangutans get to know each other before they **mate**. They spend time sharing food and cuddling! Female orangutans begin to have babies when they are 12 years old. Males fight over females. Males are not usually ready to mate until they are about 15 years old.

I mate

I attract female orangutans with my long, orange hair.

And have a new baby every three to four years.

cheek pads

throat pouch

Male orangutans like to show off. They make themselves look big and strong to keep other males away from a female that they want to mate with.

I grew big cheek pads and a throat pouch when I became an adult. My cheek pads attract females and show other males that I am fully-grown and strong.

21

How Do Orangutans Care for Their Babies?

Female orangutans are **pregnant** for eight to nine months. Then they give birth to their babies. A newborn baby is completely helpless. Its mother must look after it all the time.

I hold on tight.

SAVE THE ORANGUTAN!

Go to the Web site www.orangutan.com to find out how to raise money to help orangutans.

I had very little hair when I was born. My mother held me all the time to keep me warm. I sat up when I was two weeks old, but my arms and legs will stay thin until I learn to climb trees.

22

Until I am two years old, my mother will carry me everywhere. I sleep with her at night in her nest. She cuddles me and grooms my hair.

I cling to my mother's chest fur while she climbs in the treetops.

Baby orangutans feed on their mothers' milk. When they are three months old, they start to eat fruit and drink water from their mothers' mouths. When they are one, they eat solid food.

23

Are Orangutans Good Mothers?

A female orangutan is the most caring mother in the animal kingdom. Young orangutans sleep in their mothers' night nests until they are three to four years old. They then live with their mothers until they are about seven or eight years old. Mother orangutans teach their babies how to find food and live safely in the rainforest.

We a.

Now that I am nearly four years old, my mother feeds me chewed—up food. Sometimes I scream and shout because I would rather drink my mother's milk! By the time I am six years old, I will feed myself.

My mother carried me against her chest until I was one year old. Now that I am stronger, I can ride on her back.

arly four years old. We must now build our own night nests.

SAVE THE ORANGUTAN!

You can help baby orangutans by giving to an orangutan orphanage.

When young orangutans reach six years of age, they often spend several weeks alone in the forest without their mothers. They leave their mothers altogether when they are about seven years old.

Can Orangutans and People Live Together?

Some areas of rainforest are now **national parks** and wildlife **reserves**. Here orangutans can live safely. However, many other orangutan territories are being destroyed. That forces hungry orangutans to look for food in nearby farmlands, where they are killed by farmers protecting their crops.

SAVE THE ORANGUTAN!

Do a walk for charity **to raise money for a** conservation project **in Borneo or Sumatra.**

Some people in Borneo and Sumatra are very poor. They believe that they can make money by cutting down rainforests for wood or to make farmland.

Did You Know?

In 1997, Borneo forest fires killed a third of the orangutans there.

Lots of orangutans live in zoos. By keeping us alive in zoos people can stop us from becoming extinct. However, it is very important that there are places in the wild where orangutans can still live.

We are so much like people that we can easily catch your diseases and die.

Forest fires are sometimes used to clear rainforest to make way for farmland. Forest fires often become out of control and huge areas of rainforest burn down.

What Can You Do to Help Orangutans?

Many organizations are trying to protect orangutans in the wild. They also help orangutans that have been orphaned by forest fires or captured for the illegal pet trade.

Why not adopt me?

28

Rehabilitation centers take care of rescued orangutans. They return them to the wild as soon as they are old enough to take care of themselves. It can take many years before an orangutan is ready to be released into the wild.

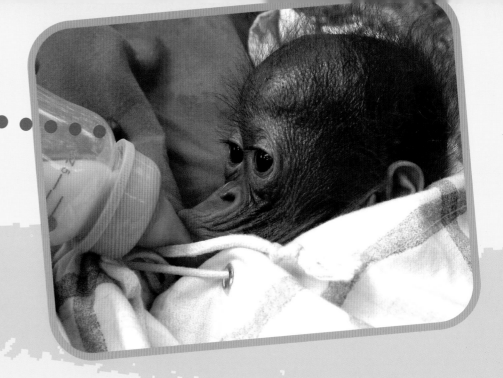

SAVE THE ORANGUTAN!

Money from visitors helps pay the costs of running orangutan orphanages. If you go to Indonesia, you can visit an orangutan orphanage.

Find out more about how you can help save orangutans and their rainforests by visiting this Web site:

www.powerkidslinks.com/savethe/orangutan/

These labels let you know that the product you are buying has been made without destroying the rainforests.

Glossary

charity (CHER-uh-tee) A group that gives help to the needy.

conservation project (kon-sur-VAY-shun PRAH-jekt) A group that tries to protect plants or animals.

environmental group (en-vy-ern-MEN-tel GROOP) A group that tries to protect the environment.

extinct (ek-STINKT) When a type of animal or plant dies out forever.

flower nectar (FLOW-er NEK-tur) A sweet, sugary liquid made by a flower.

fungi (FUN-jy) Something that lives and grows on other living or dead plants.

mammal (MA-mul) An animal that gives birth to live young and feeds them with its milk.

mate (MAYT) When a male and female animal join to make babies.

moat (MOHT) A deep hole cut into the ground so it makes a circle. Moats are filled with water.

national park (NASH-nul PAHRK) An area of land that belongs to everybody in a country.

native (NAY-tiv) A person or people whose ancestors have always lived in an area.

organizations (or-guh-nuh-ZAY-shunz)

Groups of people who work together.

orphanage (OR-fuh-nij) A place where animals whose parents have died can live.

predator (PREH-duh-ter) An animal that hunts other animals for food.

pregnant (PREG-nent) When a female animal is carrying a baby inside her.

rainforest (RAYN-for-est) Woodland where a lot of rain falls.

rehabilitation center (ree-huh-bih-luh-TAY-shun SEN-ter) A place where injured or endangered animals are taken care of.

relative (REH-luh-tiv) A person or animal that is related to us.

reserve (rih-ZURV) An area of land in which an animal can safely live.

scientist (SY-un-tist) Someone who uses science to find out more about the world.

species (SPEE-sheez) The group or type used to describe a plant or animal.

termite (TUR-myt) A small insect.

territory (TER-uh-tor-ee) The area that an animal lives in.

vegetarian (veh-juh-TER-ee-un) To only eat vegetables and no meat.

Index